'Facebook Funnies'

Over 1,000 status updates to keep your friends laughing for days!

Shelly Berryhill

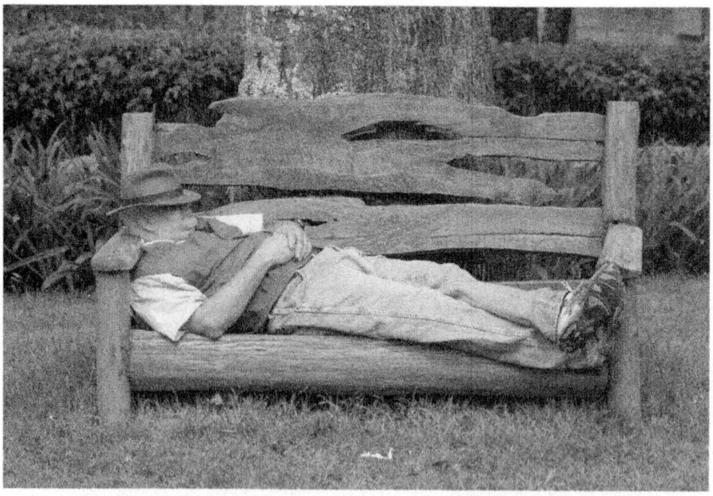

Copyright © 2017 Shelly Berryhill

All rights reserved.

http://www.shellyberryhill.com   @shellyb

DEDICATION

This book is dedicated to my children, Kristen & Kyle. They bring a smile to my face every day. Just like I hope this book does for you!

ACKNOWLEDGMENTS

I would like to thank my family for putting up with my silliness. I can't tell you how often they have rolled their eyes at my humor, but they support me anyway. My wife, Vonnie, is the love of my life. My children, Kristen and Kyle, are my reason for existing.

A special thanks to all of my Facebook friends that let me know which status messages are a home run and which ones strike out! I appreciate all 3,001 of you!

PROLOGUE

One day, several years ago, I saw or heard something that amused me. For whatever reason, I decided to post that funny on Facebook.

Well, both of my kids went ballistic! "Daddy, NO! You are embarrassing us. Don't you dare post something like that on Facebook!"

Well, all that did was put fuel to my fire. I thought, "I'll show them." So, I started posting some silliness every day. It was just my way to bug my kids. But after a while, it seemed to catch on.

If I failed to post for a day, people would call or text or email saying, "Where's my Shellyism today?" So, the journey began. Now for more than six years, I have been posting a funny to Facebook, Twitter, and Google Plus. (Yes, some of us still use Google Plus. All six of us enjoy it.)

I am often asked, "Why don't you write a book - these are hilarious." So, here is my collection of what I consider the best posts from over 6 years of funnies….

DISCLAIMER

These are NOT my original thoughts.

I have no idea where most of these funnies come from. People send them to me; I hear them; I see them on *reddit* or other people's Facebook pages.

I take no claim that these are my original thoughts. This is simply a collection of some of the funniest posts that I have seen around. If someone claims ownership of a post, please don't sue me - consider it a compliment. If you so ask, I will remove any such posts from future reprints and from the online edition.

Also, if any of these postings offend you - well that's my fault. Sometimes my humor tends to be slightly perverted. I have asked my Pastor to keep me in check - but, he seems to have more important things to do than to keep raising his eyebrows at some of my posts. So, if you enjoy this book - there are hundreds of people to thank. If you are offended, blame only me (and Pastor Jeff!).

If you're confident enough, every zoo is a petting zoo.

I have a lot of imaginary friends. They are real people; I just have to pretend they are my friends.

Seems like you could save a lot of time if you just paired The Bachelor with The Bachelorette.

I'm going to the gym because I heard they have free weights. I wonder how many they'll let me take?

If my superpower was to be able to stop time, I'd totally use it to take a nap without people noticing.

Woke up this morning and the alarm clock was laughing at me... .then I realized it was upside down and the time was 7:07

One day, long, long ago there lived a woman who did not whine, nag, or complain. But it was a long time ago, and it was just that one day.

"I went to a topless beach today. It was very disappointing. No sand whatsoever."

"The cops came to my house earlier, claiming that my dog had chased someone on a bike. I said "NO WAY, my dog doesn't have a bike!"

... keeps pressing escape but he's still here!

...is diagonally parked in a parallel universe.

...knows that God will turn your tests into your testimony!

"I had to quit my career as a skier last week. It was going downhill, fast"

...is just working here 'til good fast-food job opens up!

Well.... Here I am....What were your other two wishes?

What if I told you I could literally cut your phone bill in HALF with an exciting new product called scissors?!

Your eyes water when you yawn because you miss your bed and it makes you sad.

drove past the drug rehab center today and was rather amused by the sign out front - "Keep off the grass."

Some of us are still "it" from a childhood game of tag.

I like going into McDonald's and ordering an Egg McMuffin and a McChicken, just to see which one comes first.

Never marry a tennis player. Love means nothing to them.

My dog acts like their entire family was murdered by a vacuum cleaner.

All the guys from 'Pawn Stars' should compete on an episode of 'The Price is Right'

My insomnia is getting so bad that I can't even sleep at work.

I was kidnapped by a pack of mimes. They performed unspeakable acts on me.

Having a bit of a lazy day...sitting in my underwear looking for jobs online. My boss doesn't look amused.

I will never repeat filthy rumors. So listen closely the first time.

I have no problem giving credit when credit is due. But giving payment when payment is due is an entirely different thing.

... got a new job with the local hostage negotiators and tried to phone in sick but they talked me out of it.

The scroll to find my birth year on websites is getting uncomfortably long.

I'm usually on the outside looking in because, you know, restraining orders

I bet you $567.89 you can't guess how much I owe my bookie.

Speaking of taxation, "if you are not at the table, you are probably on the menu"

I used to be a man trapped inside a woman's body. And things got even more complicated after I was born.

is updating the expiration dates on the stuff in the fridge.

Dogs are God's way of apologizing for your relatives.

Deja-Vu ... When you're doing something you've done before, it's because God thought it was so funny, he had to rewind it for his friends.

How is it that I always seem to buy the plants without the will to live?

The most awkward part of meeting new people is when my kids say, "Please help us."

I want my children to be independent headstrong people. Just not while I'm raising them.

...*says God made butt cracks go up and down and not side to side, so when we would go down a slide it doesn't sound like this...* **blubflubblibblub**

Sometimes, I just want to go where all the missing socks go.

When you order food at a restaurant, you always start your order with a drink. At a fast food joint, you always end your order with a drink.

Somedays I feel like running away. Then I remember how much I hate running.

If Burger King married Dairy Queen, they would probably live in a White Castle.

It must suck to be a butterfly on super windy day. "Oh, I guess I'm going this way now."

I'll call it a smartphone the day I yell "Where's my phone?" and it yells "Down here! In the couch cushions!"

… 's fake plants died because he did not pretend to water them.

If your name exceeds four syllables, I'm gonna just call you "hey"

It's been an exhausting day of pretending I'm a pleasant person.

My time machine and I go way back.

The sign said 'Free Range Chickens.' So, I took three.

likes long walks, especially when they are taken by people who annoy him.

After 28 years of marriage, my wife still makes me smile. At least for the pictures.

Throughout history, there have been places where great and creative minds have gathered to become greater...this is not one of those places.

I've burned my mouth while eating a slice of pizza so, yes, I do know what it's like when a loved one betrays you.

Pizza is the most convenient food ever until you realize the box won't fit in your trashcan.

Denial, Anger, Bargaining, Depression, Acceptance... The five stages of waking up.

"I forgot to plug my car in" will eventually be the most common excuse for being late to work.

I spend a lot of time holding the refrigerator door open looking for answers.

Twitter: @shellyb   www.shellyberryhill.com

When a cashier asks if you found everything you were looking for, take their hand, look deeply into their eyes and say, "I have now."

Watched five movies on Netflix last night and now my "recommended for you" queue is "pay some bills" and "clean the bathroom"

I love how music can take you to another place. For example, One Direction is playing in this cafe so now I'm going to a different cafe.

Claiming a product promotes "Weight Loss" when combined with diet and exercise is like claiming that it grants wishes when with a leprechaun

Whoever said your harshest critic is yourself was clearly never married.

If it's the thought that counts, then I should probably be in jail...

By the time I realized my parents were right, I had kids that didn't believe me.

When you have a lot, you have hair. When you only have a few, you have hairs.

Just for fun, next time you see a snooty, rich woman at the grocery store, ask her if she works there.

I just decorated my bedroom to look like my desk at work so I can fall sleep faster.

I always like seeing those "Baby on Board" stickers because it's nice to see agreeable babies out there.

If the chemical symbol for water is H2O... is the chemical symbol for holy water H2Omg?

Remember when teachers asked to lie quietly with your head on your desk? My boss has yet to be impressed with this skill.

To understand paranoid people better, follow them around!

If you're having second thoughts, you're 2 ahead of most people.

I'm not stealing my neighbor's WiFi, their WiFi is trespassing into my house.

Braille dictionary for sale. Must see to appreciate.

Vonnie is complaining that I never buy her jewelry. In my defense, I didn't even know she sold jewelry. :-/

*Vonnie is my wife going on almost 30 years no. She is very patient with me when I use her name in my posts. She's the best!

How ignorant do I have to be before I start experiencing bliss?

Compared to Victoria's Secret, what Starbucks charges for a cup isn't that bad.

People must stop questioning my sanity, it won't answer them.

I like to think outside the quadrilateral parallelogram

Decided to make a life altering decision today.... When I think of it I'll let you know.

*If you rip a hole in a net, there's actually fewer holes in it than before! *mind blown**

My doctor wrote me a prescription for dailysex but Vonnie insists it says dyslexia.

... used to be a lifeguard, but some blue kid got him fired.

Never lie to an X-Ray technician. They can see right through you.

Vonnie asked me if I knew where the broom was. Guys, it was not a good idea to ask her if she was going somewhere.

I now own an EpiPen. My friend gave it to me when he was dying. It seemed really important to him that I have it.

If only someone on the Internet would give me their opinion on the election.

It's called fall because everything is falling... leaves, temperature, bank account, GPA, motivation...

It's actually the voices outside my head that bothers me the most.

After the expiration date on poison, is it more potent or less potent?

I WON THE LOTTERY, SCREW YOU ALL! ... Sorry, just practicing.

I wasn't planning on giving Christmas gifts this year until I heard about those exploding Samsung G7 Note phones.

Why does no one ever talk about where a bear pees?

I just walked by an old man who kept saying, "One, three, five, seven, nine... one, three, five, seven, nine..." I thought, "How odd."

Why don't we wait for life on other planets to find us? Why do we have to do all the work?

If I ask Vonnie to take a picture of me with my phone there is a 99% chance it will be a video of me yelling "It's the button on the left!"

Most people decide to have scramble eggs immediately after thinking: "I'll just flip this omelet"

I'm known all over the world for my exaggerations.

When I arrive at work, how long can I spend screaming in my car before it becomes weird?

Even if you're not successful in life, you are guaranteed to get two certificates.

Wine is just grapes for procrastinators.

I'm paying my taxes with a smile, but they wrote me back saying they want cash.

I just want to be rich enough to be referred to as eccentric instead of crazy.

I came downstairs this morning to see that my curtains were drawn......All the furniture was real though.

Last night I went to a "Testicular Cancer" survivor party. Everyone had a ball.

Got caught up in a really good book last night. I didn't stop coloring till 2 o'clock this morning.

I have removed all the unhealthy food from my house. It was delicious.

Why do we call it toilet paper? Does anyone wipe their toilet with it?

If I ever win the lottery & someone asks me for money I'm going to give them a dollar & say "Here. Go play the Lottery. That's what I did."

Twitter: @shellyb   www.shellyberryhill.com

I heard the next Steve Jobs movie will be on IMAX. It's the same movie, just on a bigger screen.

Vegetables are a must on my diet. I am eating Carrot cake, Zucchini bread and Pumpkin pie.

I don't like to make plans too far in advance because then the word "premeditated" gets thrown around in the courtroom.

I was super lazy today. Which is like normal lazy but I'm also wearing a cape.

My retirement plan is just $1,000 & a plane ticket to wherever these kids are living on 15 cents a day.

Fun thing to do: Go to a parking lot and put sticky notes on cars saying "Sorry for the damage" and watch them look for it.

Once you start making Freudian slips, you can't stop. It's just one after a mother.

Vonnie indicated she was upset with me because of my obsession with "The Monkeys." I thought she was joking....

... and then I saw her face.

You shouldn't be allowed to wear animal print if you are bigger than said animal.

If the cigarette tax is meant to discourage smoking, is the income tax meant to discourage working?

Guys in working out photos look like they're in pain, but there's lots of pictures of me with cake and I look happy. Just saying.

I know my limits. I don't pay any attention to them, but I know them

I saw a man at the beach yelling "Help, Shark!" Somehow I knew that shark wasn't going to help him.

I wear a ski mask to bed so if there is a home invasion, the intruder will think I'm part of the team.

I'll rise, but I won't shine

.

Just finished reading the fifth book in the "learning to count" trilogy.

The cashier seemed to appreciate that I bagged my own groceries until I unpacked them all and said "That's how I want you to do it"

When someone rings the doorbell, why do dogs always assume it's for them?

The voices in my head are not real, but they have good ideas.

Not sure if I want buns of steel, or buns of cinnamon.

Velcro is a rip-off.

Potatoes give us chips, French fries and vodka. Now explain how kale is popular…

I haven't owned a watch for I don't know how long.

When I wake up at night, I reach out to you, I love you not for what you look like, I love you for what you have inside - Me to my fridge

If you're a size 0, we shouldn't be able to see you.

I hate when I get to work and I'm at work.

Thanks to yesterday's chili, I can definitively tell you that there are 242 tiles in this bathroom stall.

I'm just wondering what the employees at the Weather Channel make small talk about.

Why are there never any good side effects? Just once I'd like to read a medication bottle that says, "May cause extreme sexiness."

Women only call me ugly until they find out how much money I make. Then they call me ugly and poor.

I'm really tired but it's OK. There's a nap for that.

Sometimes I wrestle with my inner demons. Other times, we just hug.

I'm one step away from being rich, all I need now is money.

I'm reading a book on anti-gravity. It is impossible to put down.

"Does my uniform make me look fat?" -Insecurity guard.

I called the incontinence hotline and got put on hold!!!

... is a secret agent...oh crap.

: Integrity is Everything. I'll sell you mine for fifty bucks.

wishes that some people wouldn't talk to me in the morning until I've had my coffee. (I don't drink coffee.)

Today, I looked at the cover of a book and judged it. So don't tell me what I can and can't do!

A handshake means something completely different to a cannibal.

I like to spend Monday morning trying to remember what I was avoiding doing at work on Friday.

...that's the last time I open the fridge before knocking. Who knew there was a salad dressing?

I saw a guy today at Starbucks. He had no smartphone, tablet or laptop. He just sat there drinking his coffee. Like a psychopath.

This healthy diet thing is dangerous. I just cut myself peeling an apple. This would have never happened to me with a Twinkie.

Ate too much salad yesterday so I'm going on an Oreo cleanse today.

I joined weight watchers last month, so far I've lost 38 dollars...

Why is maple syrup so expensive?... It grows on trees doesn't it?

The first time I got a universal remote control, I thought to myself "This changes everything."

Honesty is the best policy, but insanity makes for a better legal defense.

My auto-correct just changed "meditate" to "medicate". It knows me too well.

I'm taking my paycheck to the bank, because it's too little to go by itself.

Lots of us suffer in silence. You should try it.

I've deleted enough stupid Facebook posts to realize I should never, ever get a tattoo.

Women seem to want security. At least that's what they yell whenever I approach them.

I try to find the good in every situation. Wait. That was a typo. I meant "food." I try to find the food in every situation.

You, my friends are the reason I wake up every morning ♥ LOL JK, I have to pee.

I hate it when I'm taking a shower and the door opens and they're all "Get out of my house!"

I hope that Jessica Biel has a son someday and names him Batmo

I drive safer when there's food on my passenger seat than when there's a person sitting there.

Every novel is a mystery, if you never finish it.

My weight loss goal is to not care about the crumbs at the bottom of a Pringles can.

The hardest part about becoming vegan is having to wake up at 5:00 am to milk the almonds.

I tried to get life insurance, but they laughed and said you need a life for that...

I don't understand fast food. I've been eating it for years but I seem to be getting slower and slower.

I tried a vegan recipe book last night. It was much tastier than any of the recipes in it.

I took the battery out of the carbon monoxide detector last night. The loud beeping was giving me a headache and making me feel sick & dizzy.

Where have you been all my life? Please go back there.

Statistically, six out of seven dwarfs aren't happy.

I thought I'd try yoga to make myself more flexible, but I'm still incredibly stubborn.

If your parachute doesn't deploy, you have the rest of your life to fix it.

The best part of being a watch maker is that you get to make your own hours.

***Fifty Shades of Grey** is romantic only because the guy is a billionaire. If he was living in a trailer it would be a Law and Order episode.*

I used to think I was a man of vision. Now I'm pretty sure they're just hallucinations.

Who decided that the abbreviation for pound should be two letters not in the word?

What if the only reason you can't pass through a mirror is because you are blocking yourself?

I've been waiting all winter to complain about the summer heat.

You don't truly know someone until you see how they react to their bag of chips getting stuck in a vending machine.

Meat eaters and vegetarians both love animals. They just love them in different ways.

I was woken up again last night by the bulimic girl next door. I banged on the wall and shouted, "For God's sake, keep it down!"

My earthquake kit is just a tuxedo. Because in case of a disaster I want to look like the most important person to save.

Walmart closing 269 stores this year; putting 16 cashiers out of work.

I feel so stupid for cashing in my retirement account early. But then, I always feel stupid using the Coin star machine...

If you look like your passport picture, you probably need the trip.

My Bills are so big that I have to call them William now.

I do 5 sit ups daily. It might not sound like much, but there's only so many times you can hit the snooze button.

Days like today make me really wish they made Flintstones' Chewable Morphine.

thinks if Lincoln were alive today he'd probably say, "Aaaaahhh! Let me out this box!!!"

You can put truth in a grave, but it won't stay there; You can nail it to a cross and shut it up in a tomb, but it will rise!

I knew the Psychic was no good the moment she accepted my check.

can finally do a handstand and use facebook at the same time!

would kill for a Nobel Peace Prize.

I've woken up over 18,000 times and I'm still not used to it.

Folding clothes is just creating socially-accepted wrinkles

I like to think money wouldn't change me; yet when I'm winning at Monopoly I'm a terrible person.

If pigs could fly, I bet their wings would taste delicious.

Dog food could say it's any flavor it wants, you're not going to test it

"I stayed up all night to see where the sun went...And then it dawned on me."

If you think your wife has a sense of humor, try leaving a trail of rose petals leading to a sink full of dirty dishes.

just got his leprosy cured. High 3!

You need to be moving if you want God to show you which way to go.

The word of the day is 'condescending', but that probably means nothing to you.

I learn from the mistakes of others who have taken my advice.

When I wake up at night both extremely thirsty and having to pee, I can't help but think that my body is allocating its resources poorly.

I exaggerate more than anyone in the world.

"Don't make me regret this." -things I think when accepting a friend request.

If you feel lonely... dim all lights & put on a horror-movie. After a while it won't feel like you are alone anymore

I said I was good at making decisions. I didn't say the decisions I made were good.

Your secrets are safe with me! Odds are, I wasn't even listening.

How strange, some guy just waved half of a peace sign at me...

A friend of mine just quit his job selling computer parts. He lost his drive.

Entered what I ate today into my new fitness app and it just sent an ambulance to my house.

I can cope with voices in my head but the voices outside my head drive me crazy.

The best person to get thrown in jail with would have to be the Kool-Aid Man.

If anyone tells you, you have ADHD. Pay no attention.

I don't understand how people have to "get ready for bed." I'm always ready for bed.

I've got a bumper sticker that says "Honk if you think I am doing an excellent job driving." When I cut people off, they don't know what to do.

Kudos to guy at Starbucks that said his name was "Bueller" & left before his order was ready, leaving the barista calling him over and over.

I was going to exercise this morning, but then all the sprinkles would fall off my cupcake.

What if the only thing made in China was the sticker that said "Made in China?"

If you wash dirt from a fallen ice cube, you are washing water w/water in hope that there's only water on the water you will add to water.

Why are wedding dresses bought and tuxedos rented? The utility of each is such that it should be the other way around.

Do athletic people not know about Netflix?

TEIAM...problem solved!

There are only two days in your lifetime that are not 24 hours long.

I have an inferiority complex, but it's not a very good one.

How do we know that all the ancient Greek sculptures aren't just victims of Medusa?

is not sexist. Chicks hate that!

is not young enough to know everything.

is hypocritical; he thinks that hippopotamuses are ugly.

During the Snuggie commercial I thought it was stupid but I couldn't change the channel because I was under a blanket and my arms were cold.

used to play sports. Then he realized you can buy trophies. Now he's good at everything.

was schizophrenic once, but we're better now!

Verizon is starting to treat me like I have no shirt and no shoes.

is not old. Your music really does suck.

is saying NO to negativity

isn't worried what people think. They don't do it very often.

can handle any crisis, he has children!

is wondering: if you were going to shoot a mime, would you use a silencer?

is now realizing that that the Earth was made round so that we would not see too far down the road.

knows that midwives help people out.

is seldom misquoted by his children. In fact, they usually repeat word for word the things he should not have said.

Sorry, I got mad and said a bunch of things I meant but shouldn't have said out loud.

I really need a day between Saturday and Sunday.

Be careful when you follow the masses. Sometimes the "M" is silent.

I've finally decided to do something about my weight. Lie.

I want to lose weight, but I don't want to get caught up in one of those "Eat right and exercise" scams.

Kissing a sleeping woman in an animated Disney movie is romantic but do it on a bus and the judge doesn't agree.

I went to my doctor for my check-up. The good news- he says I'm healthy as a horse. The bad news-he uses large farm animals to describe me.

Yesterday I accidentally swallowed a bottle of food coloring. The doctor says I'm OK, but I feel like I've dyed a little inside.

I should have told Vonnie I was referring to her memory BEFORE comparing her to an elephant.

It's a bad sign when your credit card bill has a comma and your bank statement doesn't!

When I die, I want my tombstone to offer free WiFi, just so people will visit more often.

Just saw a guy using a pay phone. I can only assume he's being told where to deliver the ransom money.

I support recycling, I wore this shirt yesterday.

You know you are getting old when a bunch of annoying teenagers get murdered in a horror movie and you relate more with the killer.

If my ceiling fan could hold my weight, I'd never be bored again.

I'm not a vegetarian but I eat animals who are.

Gray hair is the human body's equivalent of low toner.

I have to be careful with my kids when I talk about the death of their mother. It's a sensitive subject and I don't want them warning her.

Why is it called tourist season if you can't shoot them!

Ban pre-shredded cheese. Make America grate again.

I'm currently developing a hand sanitizer that only kills the 00.01% of germs that the others can't kill. I'm going to make a fortune.

thinks that some mornings it's just not worth chewing through the leather straps

: Who is your lifeguard?   Mine walks on water….

is like a superhero with no powers or motivation.

is trying to throw away this Yo-Yo but it seems impossible.

How famous do you have to be to get assassinated instead of murdered?

The day is already 33% complete at 8am.

Kids that are being born now will have terrible choices in email addresses.

If you lived at 123 Fake Street, no one would ever believe you.

Do people who run know that we're not food anymore?

I'm looking up in the sky and I have no idea which cloud has all my data

The new Jungle Book movie might be confusing to today's kids who don't remember when we had jungles. Or books...

Putting a light in the refrigerator is God's way of telling us that it's okay to eat before going to bed.

Nothing embarrasses a psychic more than throwing them a surprise party.

As it turns out, I'm not an afternoon person either.

My boss told me that she will be leaving work early today.... What a coincidence! So am I!

The key to eating healthy is to avoid any food that has a TV commercial.

doubts, therefore he might be.

If you could pause time, there would be no way to measure "how long" it was paused for.

Jesus' Heavenly forecast: reign forever!

So I met an Egyptian ... they walk just like us.

My wife and I decided not to have children. The kids are taking it pretty hard.

I'd like to give a shout out to all the people who are going through an identity crisis, you know who you are... I think.

The last time I was someone's type, I was donating blood.

I saw a sign that said "watch for children" and I thought "that's a fair trade."

Hockey is more enjoyable if you pretend they're fighting over the world's last Oreo.

The lyrics, "It's the end of the world as we know it" use two pronunciations of "the" in the same line.

We should all take a moment and thank God that spiders aren't pack animals.

A waist is a terrible thing to mind.

A resume is really just a list of places I don't want to work at again.

Just about the time when you think you can make ends meet, somebody moves the ends.

Every time I watch a mountain climbing documentary, all I can think is how the true star is the cameraman.

When I'm not sleepy, I listen to some Chris Brown. That knocks me out right away.

saw a woman crying as she was buying tampons earlier. Must be going through a tough period in her life.

The boss keeps talking about a company 401k ... I don't think I can run that far!

Vonnie told me she wanted to try role reversal tonight in the bedroom... So, I told her I had a headache.

I have a love/hate relationship with strong contradictory emotions.

Sometimes it takes me a full 8 hours to get nothing done.

Dippin Dots has been the ice cream of the future for over 28 years.

Unless you fell on the treadmill, nobody wants to hear about your workout.

You could just post a picture of a random object and say it's cake and people would be super impressed.

Every Facebook memory is a reminder of how dumb I was a few years ago.

Every time I buy a pack of toilet paper it is money down the toilet.

Maybe plants are really farming us, giving us oxygen until we eventually expire and turn into mulch which they can consume.

Life would be so much better if there were piñatas strategically placed throughout my day.

Life tip: if someone comes out of a bathroom sweating, do not go in that bathroom.

My therapist goes to her therapist five minutes after I leave.

What is it about being blind that makes people want to walk their dog all the time?

She likes to call it a conversation, but mostly she's gathering evidence.

I get enough exercise by just pushing my luck.

Just picked the remote up off the floor with my foot while lying on the sofa so I guess today is leg day.

In my defense, I was left un-supervised...

The moment you empty your vacuum cleaner is the moment you become a vacuum cleaner.

*I'd much rather pay extra for priority **de**boarding than priority boarding.*

Someone just called me normal, I've never been so insulted in all my life!

Power lines are just really long extension cords.

Naked yoga in the backyard is the best way to get the neighbors to pay for that privacy fence.

Whenever you buy and eat half a chicken, you are secretly sharing a meal with a stranger.

If we're in a situation where I am the "voice of reason," then we are in a very very bad situation.

Growing up, I always thought quicksand would be a much bigger problem than it ended up being.

And then her mood ring just...exploded!

They say you're not supposed to go to the grocery store when you're hungry. It's been several days now, what should I do?

I've noticed that the squirrels are gathering nuts for the winter. Couple of my friends are missing...

Did you know that doughnuts make your clothes shrink?

I'm at my neighbor's house having the most delicious dinner. Hope I finish it before they get home!

When I go running, I usually meet new people... like paramedics.

How do I like my eggs? In a cake!

I think that a lot of conflict in the Wild West could've been avoided if architects had just made their towns big enough for everyone.

It must be very hard to be a Nigerian lawyer who specializes in international inheritance law.

I used to like my neighbors, until they put a password on their WiFi.

"Get your panties in a bunch" would make a great slogan at Costco.

The fridge is a clear example that what matters is what's inside.

I just helped a really old person put their groceries in my car.

My greatest fear is that PMS is fake and that is her real personality.

I'm not the kind of guy to distance himself from anything...

Far from it.

A positive attitude may not solve all your problems, but it will annoy enough people to make it worth the effort.

If I owned a copy store I would only hire identical twins.

I want to change my name on Facebook to "No One," so when I try to add people, it will say, "No One wants to be your friend."

Turns out the button on the elevator with the fireman's hat on it is not the button for a free fireman's hat.

Dear life, When I said "can my day get any worse?" it was a rhetorical question, not a challenge.

Toilet paper should be free and have advertising printed on it.

My New Year's resolution is to help all my friends gain ten pounds so I look skinnier.

Wow, I can't believe it's been a whole year since my herb garden was stolen. Where did the thyme go?

I find it ironic that the colors red, white, and blue represent freedom until they are flashing behind you.

Is a bath relaxing for Michael Phelps, or does he just feel like he is at work?

I may have schizophrenia, but at least I have each other.

I never finish anyth

I've spotted six Pokémon today but I don't have the game so I may need new meds...

Thanks to Facebook, I now know what everyone's bathroom looks like one mirror at a time.

I got my stomach by doing as many crunches as I can every day. Usually either Nestle or Captain.

When I want your opinion ... I'll take off the duct tape.

won employee of the month again. I love being self-employed.

If you teach sex education, it's good to tell kids the feelings they're having are normal, but funnier to single one out and mouth "Except yours."

I want to steal a doughnut truck and run because I think it'll be funny watching a bunch of cops chasing a doughnut truck on the news.

I just scrolled so far back on Facebook's Timeline it logged me back onto Myspace.

We never realize how many people we dislike until it comes to naming our child.

One day, long, long ago there lived a woman who did not whine, nag, or complain.

But it was a long time ago, and it was just that one day.

So apparently, the security guard at Kroger didn't believe that life gave me that lemon.

I can hear music coming from my printer. I think the paper's jammin' again.

Procrastination is the art of keeping up with yesterday.

Mission Impossible? He's done four of them now. Let's call it "Mission Pretty Hard but Totally Doable"

The first rule of "Condescending Club" is really kinda complex and I don't think you'd understand it even if I explained it to you.

If you get Mickey Mouse ears at Disney World, what do you get at Dollywood?

Why is it called 'after dark' when it really is 'after light'?

My doctor prescribed me some suppositories for my nausea. They're not the best medicine in the world, but they're right up there.

Voicemail should be renamed "messages from people over 40".

I have so little faith in humanity that I look both ways before crossing a one-way road.

I used to be in a band called "missing cat". You've probably seen our poster.

Don't you hate it when someone answers their own questions? I do.

Too often we spend all of our time seeking God for answers to our problems when what we should be doing is just seeking God.

I'm trying to kick dairy and now I've got the milk shakes.

Something I will never understand: Why it's acceptable for people to be idiots but not acceptable for me to point it out.

I feel like landlords who don't allow dogs but DO allow children don't know very much about children.

I always ask my waitress to name everything that comes in the salad then I respond "OK, I want a cheeseburger with none of that on it."

I think animal testing is a terrible idea; they get all nervous and give the wrong answers.

Giraffes look down on people like you.

just dropped skittles in the toilet and flushed....... it was like a 10 second Nascar race.

I have many hidden talents. Just wish I could find 'em.

No "how I made a million dollars" book starts with the author reading a book about how to make a million dollars.

You just don't see enough people being taken away in straight jackets anymore.

Teenagers are like cats. They are totally dependent on others and act like they aren't.

Until public restrooms have automatic doors, the automatic sinks, soap and paper towel dispenser will make no sense to me.

Cashiers are always checking me out.

There's no louder sound than the crunch of something you are not supposed to be eating.

A positive attitude may not solve all your problems, but it will annoy enough people to make it worth the effort.

Once again I've woken up without super powers. Sigh.

OK. So I danced like no one was watching. Anyone know a good lawyer?

I'm not sure what my spirit animal is, but I'm sure it has Rabies.

I can't decide if people who wear pajamas in public have given up on life or are living it to the fullest.

I call in sick on full moons just to make them wonder.

If cats had wings, they would still just lay there.

The mechanic asked if I wanted my tires rotated & I was like, "No thanks, I'm pretty sure they do that all by themselves while I'm driving"

My local hairdresser got arrested for selling drugs. WOW! I've been her customer for 10 years and had no clue she was a hairdresser!

Thought I'd go back through and delete some of what I think are pretty idiotic status updates... Can I have your password?

My cats always look at me like I should have planned something for us to do.

Letting the cat out of the bag is a whole lot easier than putting it back in.

I'm going paperless at home but it's presenting a real problem in the bathroom.

I wonder how many animals we had to jump on the backs of before we noticed horses were cool with it.

Relieved to finally get a new microchipped debit card that provides added security to protect the $13.68 in my checking account.

I never thought I'd be one of those people that hit the gym early in the morning.............I was right!

Becoming an adult is watching Home Alone and wondering how the parents afforded the house.

Can't find your children? Try turning off the Wi-Fi. They appear suddenly.

Does the employee manual say I CAN'T set up my camping tent inside my cubicle? No? Then please step outside and zip the door up behind you.

Does anybody know how to disable the autocorrect feature on my wife?

If I have trouble remembering every mistake I've ever made, I just pour Vonnie 3 glasses of wine.

I want to be elected president, learn the truth about aliens, and then resign.

Sometimes Google should just come back with a message that says "trust me, you don't want to know."

Vonnie woke up this morning with a HUGE smile on her face. I love Sharpie markers.

A College diploma is just a fancy receipt.

What if Ghosts try to kill you only because they want you as a friend?

I'm sorry. I know I said hi, but I wasn't really prepared for any follow-up conversation.

My dog understands what I say. I don't understand what he says. He must be much smarter than me.

Vampires are just cannibals on a juice diet.

I could be bulletproof and have no idea.

Perhaps the Navy should actively recruit more people who cannot swim; that way they will be way more determined to defend their ship.

I don't think my employer cares if I'm drug free, I think they want to know if I'll pee in a cup on command.

It's not easy being a parent these days. Texting in all caps just doesn't have the same impact as good, old fashioned yelling.

I hate people that take drugs, specially U.S. Customs and the D.E.A.

To this day, the boy that used to bully me at school still takes my lunch money. On the plus side, he makes a great Subway sandwich.

I will not sleep until I find a cure for my insomnia.

The best thing about telepathy is... I know, right!?

The invention of the shovel was groundbreaking!

While on hold for an extended period of time, you should have the option to talk with another person who is also on hold.

I joined weight watchers last month, so far I've lost 38 dollars...

Laughter is the best medicine (that my insurance is willing to cover)

I saw that my ironing board cover was all wrinkled. I laughed at the irony. Then I laughed again because irony has the word iron in it.

Gambling addiction hotlines would do so much better if ever fifth caller was a winner.

I've just won 8 straight games of Paper, Scissors, Rock, against that predictable Edward Scissorhands.

I promise I'm not stalking you! Oh, and by the way, you're out of milk.

So I turned my phone onto "airplane mode" and threw it up into the air. Worst transformer ever!

will never, under any circumstances, take a sleeping pill and a laxative on the same night again!

If robbers ever broke into my house and searched for money, I'd just laugh and search with them.

I may have schizophrenia, but at least I have each other.

Whew. Thank you, warning label. I was actually considering using my new floor lamp in the shower.

I just watched my neighbor's dog chase its tail for 10 minutes and I thought to myself, "Wow dogs are easily entertained" Then I realized, I just watched my neighbor's dog chase its tail for 10 minutes...

I like it when I buy a bag of air, and the company is nice enough to put some chips in it.

My Cousin Donna texted me and asked "what does IDK stand for?" I said "I don't know" she replied "OMG! nobody does!"

*Whoever snuck the **s** in "fast food" is a clever person.*

Does a transformer get car insurance or life insurance?

Santa goes to your house, down your chimney, and watches you while you sleep and everyone adores him. But I do it ONE time...

Dear Google: Please stop being like my wife. Kindly let me complete my sentence before you start to give me suggestions.

My girlfriend hates it when I sneak up on her. According to her lawyer, she also hates it when I call her my girlfriend.

I don't understand banks. Why do they attach chains to their pens? If I'm trusting you with my money, you should trust me with your pens.

Stalking is where two people go on a long, romantic walk together but only one of them knows about it.

I had to go on two diets because one wasn't giving me enough food.

I look at people sometimes and think... for real? That's the sperm that won?

I always hold the door open for ladies, but they never want to get in the van...

I went to the bookstore the other day to buy a "Where's Waldo" book, but I couldn't find one anywhere. Well played Waldo, well played.

I like to have sex while listening to a LIVE music album, that way I get an applause every 3 to 4 minutes.

It's scary to think nothing can kill that 0.01% germ.

My favorite part of a marathon is watching the reaction of runners who grab my plastic cup of vodka.

If you could choose between world peace and Bill Gates' fortune, what color would your Lamborghini be?

How do I approach my neighbors and tell them that their Wi-Fi isn't working properly and they might need to reset the modem?

Apparently, this guy on the street was just tying his shoe and did NOT want to play leap frog. My bad dude, my bad.

I just poured superglue into a non-stick pan. Somebody is going to be wrong.

Kids in back seats cause accidents. Accidents in back seats cause kids.

When I die, I want to die like my grandfather who died peacefully in his sleep. Not screaming like all the passengers in his car.

If I make you breakfast in bed, a simple "thank you" will suffice. None of this "how did you get in my house?" business.

There are so many scams on the internet these days, but for $19.95 I can show you how to avoid them.

On the off chance, I'm captured by cannibals, I've got a 'Best if eaten by 1975' tattoo on my neck.

Whenever my gums bleed at the dentist, she always asks me when the last time I flossed? I look at her puzzled. It was 6 months ago. She was there.

Be honest, you haven't even walked a mile in your own shoes.

The day I see a runner smiling is the day I'll consider it.

Anything unrelated to elephants is irrelephants.

My daughter just got a tattoo of a heart, a spade, a club and a diamond.

I'll deal with her later.

Don't you just hate it when people say stuff in their status that you really didn't want to know? I hate that. Anyway, I gotta go poop.

I thought putting your finger on someone's lips and saying "Shhh... Not another word" was romantic; apparently, the judge didn't think so.

I think about sex every 3.14159 seconds. I guess I'm pisexual.

Why is there a disclaimer on the Allstate Auto Insurance commercials that says "Not available in all states"?

I always put in a full eight hours at work. Spread out over the course of the week.

Saw someone try and park a car for about 10 minutes. I didn't see the person so I'm not going to assume what gender she was.

As the dog sat watching the orchestra, he stared at the conductor and thought...

"Just throw the dang thing!"

Liven up your local library by hiding all the books on anger management.

wonders.... if you don't pay your exorcist do you get repossessed?"

What do you call a bear with no teeth?

A gummy bear.

How many Apple users does it take to change a lightbulb?

None. When the bulb goes, they just replace the house.

I have OC/DC. It's just like OCD, except it really rocks!

Does my dog know I'm actually driving the car? Or does she think I'm just riding along as well?

Hunting is easier for vegans because it's easier to sneak up on plants.

I'm a pretty big rebel; I was watching PG-13 movies when I was 12.

There is a company called Kia and a company called Nokia. I'm not sure who to believe.

Life is just way too short to use one-ply toilet paper.

You know what really hurts my feelings?

Nerve damage.

I hate the part of the morning where I have to get out of bed and participate in real life.

You'll never guess who I just saw at the gas station. It was that human torch guy from the Fantastic 4 film. I tried to get his autograph, but he just kept rolling around on the floor screaming.

got up this morning, put on a shirt and a button fell off; picked up my briefcase and the handle came off. I'm afraid to go to the bathroom.

supports bacteria - it is the only culture some people have!

I hate housework! You make the beds; you do the dishes and then six months later you have to do it all over again.

Say what you will about Kristen Stewart's acting ability, But I'm willing to bet she'd kick some serious butt in a poker game.

Without ME, it's just AWESO.

I was asked to donate money to help solve the civil unrest in Egypt, but I suspect it's some sort of pyramid scheme.

was thinking about changing to a vegetarian diet...but then figured out that they run REALLY FAST...

Glue a tiny mirror over your driver's license photo so when you hand it to the police they will get confused and arrest themselves instead.

Last time I threw a Superbowl party, all people wanted to do watch was TV.

once saw a forklift lift a crate of forks. And it was way too literal for me.

I told Vonnie she was drawing her eyebrows too high. She looked surprised.

A book fell on my head yesterday.

I guess I only have my shelf to blame.

I just killed a man with a single glare. He's not dead yet, but some day he will be.

Please don't start calling me 'hero' but this lady collapsed at the grocery store and I was the first one to call for a cleanup in Aisle 3.

has a clear conscience or is that a bad memory?

I broke a mirror now I'm looking at 7 years' bad luck... but my lawyer thinks he can get me off with 3.

is a cross dresser. I get angry deciding what to wear!

wonders.... do the actors on Unsolved Mysteries ever get arrested because they look just like the criminal they are playing?

tried to join a Tourette's support group. But they told me to piss off.

Are the unmarried employees at Kraft known as Kraft singles?

I have lots of great personality traits. Or as my doctor calls them, symptoms.

What did sushi 'A' say to sushi 'B' ?

Wasabi!

Do they have zoos in Africa or is it just "outside?"

if I ever saw an amputee being hanged, I'd just yell out letters.

called the incontinence hotline and got put on hold!!!

I was in the gifted program in school too! Though my school called it "Secret Santa".

I wonder if strippers have nightmares about accidentally showing up to work in clothes?

I was making the bed this morning when I thought to myself, "That's the last time I buy a bed from IKEA".

I went to Big Lots with a $100 gift card. They just handed me the keys to the store.

I wanna meet this bridge-jumping friend my parents always complained about.

I bet cannibals were really disappointed by elbow macaroni.

never apologizes. I'm sorry but that is just the way I am...

says, "Vonnie and I have drifted closer since buying a water bed"

The reason swans mate for life is because they don't talk.

I order the club sandwich all the time, but I'm not even a member, man! I don't know how I get away with it.

I have sexdaily!!! I mean dyslexia!

If you're a size 0 we shouldn't be able to see you.

99% of people are stupid. Luckily, I'm part of the other 2%

I thought I wanted a career; turns out I just wanted paychecks.

I used to have superpowers but the psychiatrist took them away

Just once, I'd like to do something that requires a ski mask and walkie-talkies.

Why is my GPS a female voice? Women are terrible with directions.

Are we posting pictures of missing vegans on soy milk cartons yet?

We have so much in common. You want to travel... I want you to go.

My friend quit his job at McDonalds. He couldn't take it anymore. He said the boss was a clown.

hates it when you hang with MC Hammer and he won't let you touch anything!

Why do women try to talk football? Do you see me in the kitchen discussing dishwashing strategies? No. You don't.

Man, my imaginary friend just unfriended me on Facebook.

Remember being diagnosed with amnesia

That was a day to forget.

Shot my first turkey yesterday... really really scared everyone in the frozen food section... It was awesome!!!

Vonnie said we should try some role reversal in bed last night. So I said I had a headache.

You know your childhood is over when you fall asleep on the sofa and when you wake up you're still on the sofa!

I'm going to rewrite history. History.

I say, count your chickens before they hatch. If any die, just subtract those from the total. It's pretty simple.

thinks it's odd that people justify deer heads on their walls by saying they're beautiful animals. Hmmm.... I think my wife is beautiful.

is bringing sexy back... to the store for a refund!

Sean Connery's dog must get so confused when he yells for it to sit.

I'm getting to the age that if I say "DO YOU KNOW WHO I AM?" people think I forgot who I am.

I used to think I was a man of vision. Now I'm pretty sure they're hallucinations.

wishes that some people wouldn't talk to me in the morning until I've had my coffee. (I don't drink coffee.)

Exit the womb they said... Life would be great they said...

I don't have a police record but I think I have a Sting cassette tape somewhere.

My mobile phone has more computing power than all of NASA in 1969. NASA launched a man to the moon...I launch angry birds at pigs.

We need people with multiple personalities to offset all the people who have none.

is hypocritical; he thinks that hippopotamuses are ugly.

"What do we want?!" "TIME TRAVEL!" "When do we want it?!" "IRRELEVANT!"

Haunted French pancakes give me the crêpes.

Just so we're all clear, everyone here knows that when a doctor leaves the room he's just going to check WebMD, right?

remembers when I had a filter for my thoughts. Man, that was a boring day.

used to have a handle on life, but it broke.

If something's worth doing, it's worth doing rihgt.

My parents always said I was a gifted child. Turns out they meant someone left me on their doorstep in a box.

my wallet is like an onion, every time I open it-- I cry.

will try to be nicer if you try to be smarter.

was schizophrenic once, but we're better now!

CPR is the human version of blowing in to a video game cartridge hoping it'll work again.

It's important for a pastor to identify with the sufferings of his people. So periodically they should listen to their own sermons.

When I wake up before my alarm clock, I sometimes sneak up on it while it's still sleeping and yell, "HOW DOES IT FEEL, JERK?!"

And then the Doctors give me more medication.

When I was a kid I slept with a nightlight to keep away monsters who feared small, low wattage lightbulbs.

The first rule of Braille club is .::. ::. :: :.: ..:.:. ::. .. .:: ..:.: :: :.

wonders...do subliminal (send) messages (me) really (money) work?

Don't play dumb with me. That's a game you can't win.

I'm bored, think I'll go to the mall, find a great parking spot, sit in my car with my reverse lights on for a while.

my imaginary friends won't play with me.

is ashamed for what he did for a Klondike bar!

isn't worried what people think. They don't do it very often.

is retired... he was tired yesterday and he's tired again today.

I'm starting to think I'll never be old enough to know better.

So a blonde walks into a library and-

Oh, wait.

I could eat my watch, but that would be time consuming.

is what he eats... he's fast, cheap and easy.

Kidnapping? I prefer the term "surprise adoption".

It's cute that they sell family sized Oreo boxes thinking that I am gonna share them with my family.

Do you ever get the feeling that you're being watched? Because if it's bothering you, I'll stop.

I can be as co-dependent as you want me to be.

Gravity always get me down.

missed winning the lottery by only SIX numbers!

can handle any crisis, he has children!

I wonder if anyone has watched Storage Wars and said, "Hey, that's my stuff!"?

I don't like people who can't make fun of themselves. It means more work for me.

Why don't skeletons fight each other?

They don't have the guts.

A movie ticket for a baby should cost at least $50.

My death bed confession is going to be epic!

You know you're fat when you sit in the bath and the water in the toilet rises.

is wondering: Is it true that cannibals don't eat clowns because they taste funny?

You trust me holding your child? Do you know how many iPhone screens I've cracked?

Ever had one of those days where everything goes according to plan and turns out great......yeah me neither.

I bet batteries have really low self-esteem. They're never included in anything.

I totally take back all those times I didn't want to nap when I was younger!

is wondering: if you were going to shoot a mime, would you use a silencer?

I have OCD and ADD. That means everything must be perfect, but not for very long.

I never understand when people say that the Mona Lisa was Leonardo da Vinci's best work. He was pretty good in Titanic if you ask me.

Ever talk to someone so stupid that you can hear them misspelling words?

The word "listen" contains the same letters as the word "silent".

Time flies when you're throwing watches.

Thanks, confirmation email telling me I've successfully unsubscribed from your emails. You just had to win, didn't you?

The power went out thus no internet It was raining so I couldn't play tennis. I spent 5 hours talking to Vonnie. Turns out she's pretty cool!

knows that midwives help people out.

is seldom misquoted by his children. In fact, they usually repeat word for word the things he should not have said.

The easiest way to find something lost around the house is to buy a replacement.

Running toward my dreams, tripped over reality and hit my head on the truth.

Iron Man is a superhero. Iron Woman is a command.

My Jewish friend said I used a word out of context. I hate arguing Semitics.

Look you asked me to be your child's Godfather so don't get mad at me because I taught him how to break knees and collect debts.

I have kleptomania, but when it gets to bad I take something for it.

I'm moving to Jamaica to become a hairdresser. Quite frankly I'm dredding it.

would be more willing to accept people for who they are if they were more like how I wanted them to be!

thinks that the gene pool could use a little chlorine.

The NSA is the only branch of the government that actually listens to people.

I hate when I'm singing along to a song and the artist gets the words wrong.

Life's hard for Erectile Dysfunction sufferers. Oh the irony...

My career plans were much more exciting when I was five!!!!

If you ever feel useless, remember that there are referees at a WWE match.

I think it's great that there's finally a woman in charge of the Fed. We can pay her less, right?

I don't know which is more annoying. The new self-service check-out at my local Walmart, or all the weirdos that watch me shouting at it.

I have CDO, it's like OCD but all the letters are in alphabetical order AS THEY SHOULD BE.

*A man goes into a library and asks for a book on ironic midget jokes.
The librarian says "It's on the top shelf"*

broke his iPhone using the "Bathroom Scale" app.

My level of sarcasm is to a point where I don't even know if I'm kidding or not.

Frankly, I'm used to being ignored—I'm married AND have a cat.

Guy pulled a knife on me. I knew he wasn't too serious because it had butter on it. Still for a second I thought I was toast.

I finished reading 'The Neverending Story' last night, so myth busted, I guess

Hair salons make me sad. I keep thinking of all the people who dyed there.

knew it would be in the last place he looked for it, so he looked there first.

stopped to think and forgot to start again.

The phrase, "Don't take this the wrong way", has a zero percent success rate.

I'm feeling about as useful as a stoplight in Grand Theft Auto.

I need a 6-month vacation, twice a year.

My 14-year-old son is glued to the TV. It's hilarious, I've also superglued the dog to the window.

If you want to get your kids attention, just sit on the couch and look comfortable.

is planning on living forever. So far so good.

Vonnie loves sales. She'll buy anything that's marked down. Yesterday she came home with an escalator.

Dear Warner Brothers: Now that I'm an adult, I feel I am old enough to hear what the "Beep Beep" is hiding when Road Runner talks to Wile!

I often confuse reptiles and amphibians. Actually, if I'm being honest, they pretty much never know what I'm talking about.

I live life on the edge. When I go grocery shopping, I place all of my eggs in the same basket. That's just how I roll.

is out of his mind - back in five minutes.

Calm down check out guy, you don't have to inspect my $20 so hard, If I was talented enough to make my own, I wouldn't be in Quickie Mart.

Climate: What you do with a ladder.

I want to be something really scary for Halloween. So, this year, I'm dressing up as a phone battery at 3%.

"I was cooking the other day when I got herbs in my eye, Now I'm parsley sighted". Don't worry, it will heal in thyme!

likes being vague, because it's almost as fun as doing that other thing.

They call them heated seats because rear defroster was already taken.

You will become way less concerned with what other people think of you when you realize how seldom they do.

Eating a bowl of generic frosted flakes... THEY'RRRRRRRRREEE alright, I guess.

*I went to a topless beach today.
It was very disappointing. No sand whatsoever.*

is pleading contemporary insanity!

It's getting warm out. I can finally get back to smacking people and blaming it on mosquitoes!

The Spanish word for "wife" (esposa) also means handcuffs (esposas).

While driving home yesterday I had an accident with a magician. It wasn't my fault though ....he came out of nowhere

always wanted to be somebody. Now he realizes that he should have been more specific.

is wondering: Since light travels faster than sound, is that why some people appear bright until you hear them speak?

I like to finish other people's sentences because my version is better.

If you've never used duct tape to hold on part of a car, I don't understand your kind of wealth.

My car has heated seats, and even a heated steering wheel. But only in the Summer.

Mental note: Actual notes work better.

My main goal in life is to find out what my main goal in life is.

Er... that was easy.

*The new watch I bought has no hands.
To be fair, it is made by Guess.*

Today I learned that not all people like ventriloquists. Particularly my proctologist.

I always thought it strange that Spiderman's alter ego works as a journalist. Shouldn't he work in web design?

I don't like thinking before I say something. I like to be just as surprised as everyone else by what comes out of my mouth.

A good friend of mine works at an aquarium. The screensaver on his laptop is a bunch of people in an office walking around filing stuff.

avoids alliterations always!

realized he was dyslexic when he went to a toga party dressed as a goat

I just saw an ad on Craigslist from a woman in search of "breastfeeding equipment." Weird. I thought that she should already be equipped.

I think my problem is that I have really fantastic bad ideas...

I'm so good at sleeping that I can do it with my eyes closed.

I haven't seen any new Bigfoot pictures in a while...I hope he's okay.

Being told that there is a cure for dyslexia is music to my arse.

Last night, I explained to Vonnie how twitter works. "I don't follow you", she said.

the cops came to my house earlier, claiming that my dog had chased someone on a bike. I said "NO WAY, my dog doesn't have a bike!".

hasn't got a big belly, he's got a protective covering for his rock-hard abs.

I think my mailman is stealing my Nigerian lottery checks.

Did you ever hear about that movie "Constipation"?

It never came out.

Oxymorons are basically complicated.

I think I may have lost my voice... But there is no way of telling.

If you watch 'Jaws' backwards, it's about a huge shark that throws up so many people that they need to open a beach.

is wondering: Why does the sun come out during the day, when it would be so much more useful if it came out at night when it was dark?

I prefer Subway at lunch because they make me feel like I'm making the healthy decision when I order a loaf of bread with 18 meatballs on it.

always wears a seatbelt. It makes it harder for aliens to suck him out of his car.

I'm not lazy, I'm in energy saving mode.

What do you call sad coffee?

Despresso.

I saw a poster that said "have you seen this man?" With a number to call... So, I called the number & told them "No."

*"I don't believe any of the rumors about radiation levels in Japan".
Said my sushi this afternoon.*

"Be yourself" is about the worst advice you can give some people.

is careful about reading health books... he may die of a misprint.

thinks that even if the voices aren't real, they've got some great ideas!

I just fell down the stairs with my guitar in my hands and I accidentally wrote a One Direction song.

What do you call a man with no body and just a nose?

Nobody nose.

Of course, women have cleaner minds than men. They change them much more often.

Sometimes it takes me 8 hours to get nothing done.

The older I get the more I find the Grinch to be a reasonable guy.

Finally, my Christmas shopping is complete. Now, what to get everybody else...

I'm pretty sure I'm only entertaining myself here.

My wife is adorable, smart, sexy, and looking over my shoulder as I type.

I've just had to buy ten new pets. I'm running out of passwords.

If you watch Jeopardy backwards, Alex Trebeck is really a genius!

is REALLY annoyed. I got asked to leave Harvey's supermarket for doing what one of their stupid signs said: "Wet Floor".

is sorry if he looks interested; he's not.

3 things I don't like:
1. Focusing on things I don't like

2. Lists

3. Irony

Work hard in silence, let your success be your noise.

I can't believe that every time I travel, I'm sat next to the most obnoxious family ever. But they keep insisting on coming with me.

I don't have a bad handwriting. I just have my own font.

Half the journey is knowing where you're parked.

Few things in life are more pleasurable than turning off the lights in a public bathroom while people are still inside.

Amazon is selling a book called "Test Your Dog's IQ." Presumably, if you buy it for $9.95, it's considerably higher than your own.

At what age is it appropriate to tell my dogs they're adopted?

says don't you hate those moments of awkward silence? umm... anyone?

Without Mister T, "I pity the fool" would sound like something out of a Shakespeare play.

Time zones sound a lot cooler than they actually are.

I have never seen a pie cooling on an open windowsill in person.

Any time I lift a heavy object with another person I always feel like I'm only doing 10% of the work.

Buying a new laptop from your old laptop is like making someone hire their own hitman.

In my defense, your honor, he had the keyboard clicking sound on his phone turned on.

You know you're lazy when you get excited about canceled plans.

My Internet went down yesterday. I think my neighbor forgot to pay their bill.... How irresponsible!

"Did you ever notice that when you put the words "The" and "IRS" together, it spells "THEIRS?!"

So two antennae got married. The wedding was awful but the reception was great!

can't understand why constipated people don't seem to give a crap.

says, "I am related to people that sometimes I just don't relate to.?"

What's the point of being cool if you can't wear a sombrero?

Trying to understand women is like trying to smell the color 8.

If you have a tattoo on your face, you've lost the right to ask me what I'm looking at.

Once you start making Freudian slips, you can't stop. It's just one after a mother.

Just once I want my skills to be so urgently required that a helicopter is dispatched to pick me up.

The difference between my "walking" and my "running" is mostly just arm movements.

I got fired from my job. My colleagues found out I don't really have Tourette's.

When you see a mosquito landing on your testicles, you realize that there is always a way to solve problems without using violence.

*My wife said she's sick of my childish obsession with sci-fi films.
I said, "Out on your way, the door you must close".*

is wondering: If we're not supposed to have late night snacks.. why is there a light in the fridge?

My neighbors are listening to some awesome music this morning. I hope that they don't ask me to turn it down.

I hate when I lose things at my job like my pen and self-motivation.

Happiness is using an ATM and finding a receipt left behind by someone with an account balance lower than yours.

Lying in bed, listening to the Doors. I really should oil the hinges.

I went into the local library and asked if they had any books on the Titanic.

"Oh yes, quite a few", the Librarian said. "Sorry to hear that", I replied. "They'll all be ruined by now".

Sometimes I question my sanity....only very rarely does it reply.

is Trying To Throw Away This Yo-Yo But It seems Impossible.

is the boss (Vonnie said I could be)

is like a superhero with no powers or motivation.

All the guys from 'Pawn Stars' should compete on an episode of 'The Price is Right'

Sometimes I spend whole meetings wondering how they got the big meeting table through the door

When I'm bored I like to call in sick to places I don't work for. I'm getting written up at Kohls.

Don't anthropomorphize computers. They hate that.

Note to vegetarians: My food poops on your food. Enjoy that salad!

says, "If you can't prove it, I didn't do it!"

Make yourself indispensable at work by hiding everything.

I'm a social vegan. I avoid meet.

Arkansas is just Kansas with pirates.

Google has severely diminished the chance that I will ever just take your word for it that you know something.

heard on the news that someone checked into the psych ward wearing a thong & riding a goat. I`ll come get you this time BUT this kinda stuff has to stop

I wonder if Auto Correct and Spell Check get together behind our backs and talk about what idiots we are.

Ten years ago I became a proud parent. Kristen is 24 but she was kind of a pain those first 14 years.

The only difference between an oral and a rectal thermometer is the taste!

bought some powdered water, but I don't know what to add.

I'm not usually one to brag, but I was able to get my daily recommended calorie intake down in just one sitting tonight!

I just read that 99% of all women don't like men in leather pants. That's a good thing because 99% of men in leather pants don't like women.

When comforting someone who is illiterate, I always say softly, "There, their, they're."

I just came up with a great dessert recipe. Cut up some bananas, apples & oranges in a bowl. Add fresh squeezed lime juice. Then toss it in the trash and eat a cheesecake.

"I ran a half marathon" sounds so much better than "I quit halfway through a marathon".

I wonder if the Three Wise Men said to Jesus, "Just to be clear, these gifts are for your birthday AND Christmas."

I hate it when people steal quotes from movies. It makes me angry, and you wouldn't like me when I'm angry.

wonders what would happen if he walked through Sea World with a fishing pole?

has two ways of arguing with women. neither one works.

Dating tip:
When you are on a first date and she says to you, "I want you to treat me like a movie star," it is vitally important to establish which type of movie.

I'm not usually one to brag, but I was able to get my daily recommended calorie intake down in just one sitting tonight!

No one deals with rejection more than Internet Explorer requesting to be your default browser.

I bet half of online arguments could be prevented if people had to put their age next to things they post.

Whenever I'm getting a haircut, I hope the barber is impressed with how perfectly still I sit.

I quit my job at the helium factory today. I refuse to be spoken to in that tone of voice.

I don't think I could ever stab someone.. I barely can get the straw into a Capri Sun.

once read a book about anti-gravity. I just couldn't put it down.

so appreciates your point of view that he almost regrets dismissing it

At my age, I don't take naps outdoors. People start breaking out the shovels.

I'm emotionally constipated. I haven't given a crap in days...

I always advise people never to give advice..

You sure Osama Bin Laden is dead? I'm sure he just drove me to the airport.

is the National Spellling Bee Runer-Up

was born free... but he's higher priced now

Perhaps I should reduce my consumption of butter. I like butter on almost everything: bread, corn on the cob, french fries, Skittles.....

If the body is a temple, mine must be a megachurch.

I just scraped the chocolate icing off of my doughnut. Dieting is so difficult.....

I broke my arm in two places, so I won't be going back to those places.

I wonder how long I would remain on hold if my call WASN'T important to them?

A person with a watch knows what time it is. A person with a watch, a smartphone, and a Fitbit is never really sure.

Lies are like cockroaches. If you see one, there are others.

You know you've reached middle age when all you exercise is caution.

I don't trust anyone who chooses a side salad over French fries.

Considering that dogs pee to mark territory, they probably think humans are constantly battling over who gets to claim the toilet.

If no one comes from the future to stop you from doing it.... then how bad of a decision can it really be?

They say that one in every seven friends has OCD.
It's not me.
It's either Arnold, Ben, Charles, Dennis, Edward or Frankie.

thinks your baby is beautiful. Really, I do. I'm just worried about what might happen if it gets wet, or eats after midnight...

wonders if you heard about the corduroy pillows? They're making headlines!

The saying goes "If you can't say anything nice, then don't say anything at all."....Well I guess today will be another silent day for me.

Since my ear surgery I haven't heard from my doctor. Not sure if that's a good thing or not.

Some people are wise, some are otherwise..

I was overjoyed when a letter from my Psychiatrist told me I no longer needed treatment.

"Thanks!", I said.

"No problem", it replied.

After winning my latest match, I decided to throw the ball into the crowd, like they do on TV.

Apparently it's unacceptable in ten pin bowling.

isn't "stalking" you, I'm simply following your live-action Twitter feed from a ladder outside your window.

is frustrated that he knows all the answers, but nobody bothers to ask him the questions.

Women should have one of those mood ring stones glued to their forehead.

I donate blood 5 times a year just so I'm less and less related to some of my relatives

Creative marketing is when a company owns 15 donut shops and 4 weight-loss clinics.

Every semicolon I have ever used has been a shot in the dark.

Cereal is the sweatpants of food.

IKEA meatballs contain horse DNA...

There's a joke in there somewhere, you'll have to assemble it yourselves.

is stamping out, eliminating and abolishing redundancy!

I don't have time to tell you how wrong you are. But I'm going to any way because it will bug me if I don't.

A single cow can make 400 hamburgers.

That's amazing - they should hire them as cooks at McDonald's.

Workout Journal Day #5: Jogging with a stroller is great exercise! And hard work for whoever is pushing me

asked people if they thought there were to many aliens in the U.S. ---17% said yes, 23%said no the other 60% said No Hablo Engles

thinks copy & paste is the greatest invention ever thinks copy & paste is the greatest invention ever thinks copy & paste is the greatest..

Roadside sobriety tests are getting ridiculous. Last night I had to fold a fitted sheet.

Someone just threatened to sue me for intellectual malpractice.

It's called "Biscotti" because nobody would buy "chocolate covered croutons".

I'm not saying it's hot in my house today, but two hobbits just walked past and threw a ring in the window.

I puked in the backseat of my friend's Mustang in the Fall of 1979. There wasn't any social networking back then, so I'm telling you now.

I guess I prefer Subway because they make me feel like I'm making a healthy decision when I order a loaf of bread with 18 meatballs on it.

You know that feeling when you exercise so much you can hardly move? I sometimes wonder what that feels like.

says "Give me ambiguity or give me something else."

I went to the gym this morning. It was my 2nd time GO ME! The first time I signed up. The second time I renewed.

I'm at the age where an "all-nighter" just means I didn't have to get up to pee.

Bondage...it's knot for everyone.

I don't understand fast food. I've been eating it for years but I seem to be getting slower and slower.

You owe it to yourself to become successful. After that, you'll owe it to the IRS.

Kristen told me that she won't bring her friends to the house because she was fed up with my bad habits. I nearly choked on my toenail.

wonders if illiterate people get the full effect of Alphabet Soup?

is dyslexic which means never having to say that you're yrros.

There is NO way to tell how many Chameleons are in the room right now!

Remember that the bridge you drive over today was built by the lowest bidder.

I'm an only child, and I'm still not the favorite.

I'm guessing that the actual process of giving birth is what led to the extinction of the unicorn.

I just learned today that bacteria is not the back door of a cafeteria!

...This mushroom walks into a bar and starts hitting on this woman... She, of course, turns him down. Not willing, to give up, he pleads with her... "C'mon lady, I'm a fun guy..."

was woken up again last night by the bulimic girl next door. I yelled over at her and shouted, "For goodness sake, keep it down!".

Astronauts are tweeting from space and I can't get reception from my basement.

1997: Don't trust anyone on the Internet, don't get in stranger's cars. 2017: Use the Internet to get in a stranger's car.

We live in a world where lemonade is made from artificial flavors and furniture polish is made from real lemons.

When I procrastinate, current me really expects a lot out of future me.

Dog food could say it's any flavor it wants, you're not going to test it.

If cats had wings, they'd still just lay there.

I wonder if I'll ever have to write Earth at the bottom of a postal address.

Phones should have a guest mode. If someone ever needs to use your phone, you could enter a separate passcode to ensure privacy.

Why are aliens always portrayed as being naked? If we landed on a different planet we would be wearing at least something

Brain surgery is just a bunch of brains trying to help another one out.

Yawning is like the body's "20% battery remaining" warning.

Because light has a speed, your mirror image is your past self.

My dog understand several human words. I don't understand any dog barks. He may be smarter than me.

If James Bond is the most famous spy, doesn't that make him the worst spy?

GPS says "estimated time", I see "time to beat".

The oldest person alive has lived through the birth of everyone on Earth today.

If mosquitoes sucked fat, not blood, the world would be perfect.

If a ghost is trying to kill you, does he want you as a friend?

"LSD causes users to lose weight." Obviously. You can't eat when a dragon is guarding the fridge.

Winnie the Pooh stars two kangaroos and a rabbit, yet the tiger is the one known for bouncing.

The reason why Mickey Mouse has a pet dog (Pluto) is to keep cats away.

I always say "morning" instead of "good morning" because if it was a good morning I would still be in my bed not talking to people.

The "twen" in twenty is just two and ten combined.

Why don't bags of dog food have a toy at the bottom?

If 666 is evil, then 25.806975801127 is the root of all evil.

Once you've read the dictionary, every other book you read is just a remix.

What if the "monster" under your bed sees you as the monster on top of the bed, and is so terrified he keeps as still and quiet as possible.

I just realized that the division symbol, ÷ , looks like a fraction with the dots representing the numbers.

If you clone yourself, and your clone kills you, is it suicide or murder?

Noses are in the middle of our faces because it's the scenter.

Technically, all national anthems are country music.

I didn't sleep last night so this morning I made my coffee with Red Bull. I got half way to work before I realized I forgot my car

My background check bounced.

The Voice could've saved some money on spinning chairs if they just got Stevie Wonder and Ray Charles as judges....

I was once in a band called The Stepchildren. A lot of people pretended to like us.

Building a tree house is the biggest insult to a tree. "Hey, I killed your friend. Here, hold him."

When you're smiling to the camera, you're really smiling to someone in the future.

Darth Vader could fall asleep in Imperial meetings and nobody would notice.

If you have a parrot and you don't teach him to say "Help, they turned me into a parrot" you wasting everybody's time

Humans require an 8 hour charge for only 16 hours of battery life

If dentists make their money from bad teeth, why do we use toothpaste that they recommend?

I don't think I've ever seen a "plus-size" male model

The last time I was someone's type, I was donating blood.

The word "swims" is the same upside down

The side effects list for sleep medication essentially say, "We'll put you to sleep, but we can't guarantee you'll wake up."

Fire trucks are actually water trucks.

When you drink alcohol, everyone says you're an alcoholic. When you drink fanta, no one says you're fantastic.

Have you ever realized that anything Vin Diesel eats can be considered as diesel fuel.

will never again play leapfrog with a unicorn.

walked down a street where the houses were numbered 64k, 128k, 256k, 512k and 1mb. That was a trip down memory lane.

Dear Math, I am sick and tired of finding your x. Just accept the fact that she is gone. MOVE ON, DUDE -.-

Apparently, this dude at the mall was just tying his shoe and did NOT want to play leap frog. My bad, dude. My bad.

Yesterday I had to screw in a light bulb. Later, I crossed a road and walked into a bar. My life is a joke.

Thinks the only difference between my job and the Titanic is the Titanic at least had a band!!

According to my current parking spot, I am now a physician.

I saw a guy earlier this morning that had no chin. All I can think about now is how does he put on pillow cases?

If Crunch Berries aren't considered fresh fruit, I don't believe this diet is going to work.

Perhaps I should reduce my consumption of butter. I like butter on almost everything: bread, corn on the cob, French fries, Skittles.....

I broke my arm in two places, so I won't be going back to those places.

Have you ever seen a baby horse trying to stand for the first time? That's what I look like getting out of bed in the morning.

The first rule of Vegan Club apparently is to tell everyone about Vegan Club.

I just burned 1200 calories! I forgot about the pizza in the oven.

dyslexic means never having to say you're srroy

A hamburger walks into a bar, the bartender says, "sorry, we don't serve food in here"

does not believe in superstition. It brings bad luck.

I, put commas, in, weird places, so that, you, will, read, this, like William, Shatner.

Eating 4 cans of alphabet soup will give you a giant vowel movement.

If any illiterates are reading this, you're probably not.

My desktop could be on Hoarders.

only hates the people in front of me while checking out at the store. Everyone behind me is cool.

is known for his motivational skills. Everyone says they have to work twice as hard when I'm around.

doesn't have issues - he has volumes!!

I used to be poor, then I bought a dictionary. Now I'm impecunious.

I wonder how long it will take this police sketch artist to realize I'm describing him.

I don't want to be a millionaire, I just want enough money to be able to stare off into the distance while pumping gas.

Of course Bruce Willis is gonna keep playing the same movie roles. You know what they say about old habits..

I nevur make the same mistake twice. NEVUR.

is walking through the intensive care unit dressed as the grim reaper

Apparently putting Alka-Seltzer in my mouth while getting baptized and pretending I'm being possessed by the devil is not funny.

If people in horror movies listened to me, they'd still be alive!

If you have a bladder infection you know Urine trouble

Whatever you do, always give 100%. Unless you're donating blood.

I'm guessing that most people who claim to "count calories" are really bad at math

understands that if Satan ever loses his hair, there will be hell toupee.

says my computer just beat me at chess...but it was no match for me at kick boxing

Any dog can be a guide dog if you don't have any particular destination.

Rappers act all hard but all they're doing is reading you their poetry.

The older a man is, the less I question his choice of a hat.

I love to give homemade gifts. Which one of my kids do you want?

I wish I had somebody to blame all of my problems on, like my wife does.

Vonnie told me to see things from a woman's point of view, so I looked out the kitchen window.

I have a mental disorder that causes me to make everything I say sound mysterious.

Or do I?...

thinks a city built on rock 'n roll would be structurally unsound.

dreams of a better world...where chickens can cross the road without having their motives questioned

I was watching the kids play hide and seek in the park yesterday and my friend's kid hid behind a chain link fence. The positive thing is at least he doesn't have to save for college.

Starting tomorrow, every place that I visit, I'm going to speak exclusively in double negatives. I'd do it today, but I'm not going nowhere.

It wasn't until I tasted the chewy monkey bits through the chocolate & peanut butter that I realized I accidentally bought Rhesus Pieces.

I don't swim because it's never 30 minutes after the last time I ate.

When people with lisps say "Bithneth", you know they mean business.

Candy corn is just like regular corn except it dances on poles and has self esteem issues.

So there are these "Don't start forest fires" commercials telling me to "Get my Smokey on." All I can think is, if an anthropomorphic bear in a pair of jeans and a ranger hat comes up and tells me not to set stuff on fire, I probably already did.

Would it be wrong to refer to a man in a dress, with a hearing aid, smoking a joint, as a High Deaf TV?

Whenever someone invites me to their home and I see more than 3 cars parked outside, I keep driving just in case it's an intervention.

Ironically the only way I'd watch the 50 Shades of Grey movie is if you tied me to a chair and forced me to.

Turns out, I'm not an afternoon person either...

I live by my own rules (reviewed, revised, and approved by my wife).. but still my own

My grandfather worked in a steel fabrication plant. They didn't produce anything, they just said they did.

remembers when shopping for cereal was a lot more fun when you cared about the toy instead of the fiber

I'm taking up photography because it's the only hobby where I can shoot people and cut off their heads without going to jail.

I'm probably not going to get accepted into the optimist club.

I was going to start jogging today, but then I remembered that I own a car.

Old is when ... An "all nighter" means not getting up to pee!

I fell off a 50ft ladder today... Luckily I was only on the bottom step.

I just watched 'The Curious Case of Benjamin Button' for the third time.

Never gets old.

took the "How gullible are you?" quiz. He must have done well...when he was done, it asked for his bank account # to deposit his prize.

I'm not insulting you, I'm describing you.

Technically, every picture is a before picture.

I have a fear of speedbumps, but I'm slowly getting over them.

Whenever I ride on a roller coaster, I bring some nuts and bolts with me. Right before the ride starts I say to the person beside me, "OH NO! These came off your seat!!!"

Thinks I'm gonna entertain my kids with a nice game of duct, duct tape

ate 3.14159265358979323846ths of a pie.

I just poured superglue into a non-stick pan. Someone is going to be wrong.

Judging by the taste of Special K cereal, I can only imagine how terrible Normal K cereal must taste.

I was watching the kids play hide and seek in the park yesterday and my kid hid behind a chain link fence. The positive thing is at least I don't have to save for his college fund.

The only thing that appears correct on my paycheck is the amount I got paid is "gross."

I hate the part of the morning where I have to get out of bed and participate in real life.

If I ever put stuff in storage I'm going to write "gold bars" and "priceless memorabilia" on the boxes just to mess with storage wars.

finds it ironic that the Alzheimer's Association is sponsoring an event called 'A night to remember'.

has had amnesia for as long as he can remember

is: going to make hermit crabs live together

I know my job is secure because no one else wants it.

You can't trust atoms. They make up everything.

Got pulled over today for "texting while driving". Stupid cop! I wasn't texting. I was playing Words With Friends.

On any given day in a hospital, you can find people having the best day of their life, the worst day of their life, the first day of their life, and the last day of their life all under one roof.

When I wake up at night both extremely thirsty and having to pee, I can't help but think that my body is allocating its resources poorly.

Do Starbucks employees take coffee breaks?

I used to think I was good at multi-tasking. Turns out it's just my multiple personalities doing one task at a time.

Is it just me or is CSI just like Scooby Doo but for old people?

thinks that the person that designed the stick figures on the back of everyone's minivan is probably the millionaire I hate the most.

~ A jumper cable walks into a bar, and looks around aggressively at the other customers. The bartender says, "All right, I'll serve you.... but don't start anything."

is wondering why, if the #2 pencil is so popular, is it still #2?

People who help you find what you are looking for in a liquor store should be called Spirit Guides.

Technically every mirror you buy at a store is in used condition.

Birth certificates are basically receipts for humans.

Revenge is a dish best served cold. Revenge is sweet. Revenge is probably ice-cream.

Telephone poles are just trees with jobs.

I wish we lived in a world where I can order mozzarella sticks, and not get judged or questioned when I ask the waiter to put cheese on them

THE AUTHOR

Shelly J. Berryhill is first and foremost a Christian. He said, "Christ died so that I might live. That is the most important characteristic of my life."

He is also a politician (local city commissioner), and a real estate appraiser. Berryhill is a self-proclaimed geek by nature and an early adopter of technology. A 1982 graduate of Hawkinsville High School in Hawkinsville, Georgia, he is a 1986 graduate of the Georgia Institute of Technology.

Berryhill says, "I love to smile. I hope you enjoy this book as much as I have enjoying posting over the years." If you found it enjoyable, post a comment at www.shellyberryhill.com or give us a good Amazon review or send me a tweet!

Printed in Great Britain
by Amazon